French
Revision

Gill James

Good day. I'm Sir Ralph Witherbottom. I'm an accomplished inventor, a dashing discoverer and an enthusiastic entrepreneur.

Hi! I'm Isabella Witherbottom – my friends call me Izzy. I'm Sir Ralph's daughter and I like to keep him on his toes!

And they both keep me on my toes! How do you do? I'm Max, the butler, at your service.

Woof! I'm Spotless – aptly named, as you can see. I'm the family's loyal dog.

Contents

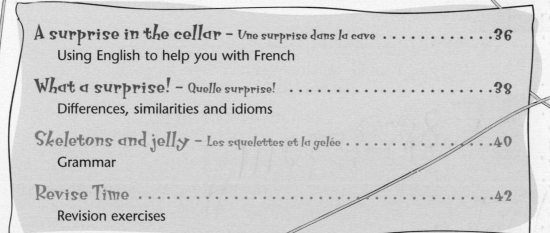
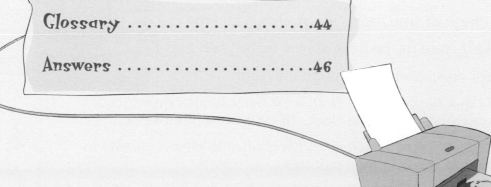

The speaking clock
L'horloge parlante

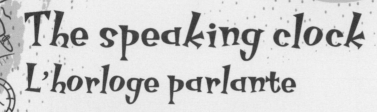

Sir Ralph Witherbottom had made a clock that said the time in French when you pressed a button on it. The problem was, though, that sometimes it told you the time when you had not even asked it!

"**Il est huit heures trente**," said the clock.

"Eight thirty already," said Sir Ralph. "Time I started my work."

"Il est **dix** heures **quarante-cinq**," said the clock later.

"Quarter to eleven," said Isabella Witherbottom. "Time for coffee, I think."

"Il est **treize** heures **cinq**," said the clock.

"Lunch is five minutes late today," said Max, the butler. "Sorry that it wasn't ready for one p.m. as usual!"

"Il est **quatorze** heures **quinze**," said the clock.

"Yes," said Isabella, "quarter past two. Time for me to visit Armelle."

"Il est **seize** heures **vingt**," said the clock.

"Twenty past four," said Max. "Time for Spotless' walk."

"Il est **dix-neuf** heures **cinquante-cinq**," said the clock.

"Good," said Sir Ralph. "The eight o'clock news is on in five minutes and Izzy should be home too."

Dix-huit heures dix? Time for supper, I think!

"Il est **vingt et une** heures **vingt-cinq**," said the clock.

"Five minutes before my bedtime at nine thirty," said Isabella.

The clock kept on speaking all through the night.

"Il est vingt-deux heures trente-cinq, il est deux heures quarante, il est trois heures vingt," said the clock. "Il est quatre heures dix."

The Witherbottoms were woken up at twenty-five to eleven, twenty to three, twenty past three and ten past four.

The next day, a rather tired Sir Ralph decided it was best to dismantle the clock!

What time does it mean?

Match the times on these two lists.

1	Il est quinze heures cinq.	Quarter to two in the afternoon.
2	Il est neuf heures dix.	6.30 p.m.
3	Il est vingt heures vingt.	Five past three in the afternoon.
4	Il est dix-huit heures trente.	Ten past nine in the morning.
5	Il est treize heures quarante-cinq.	Twenty past eight in the evening.

Top Tips!

You can write times down in figures. Where we put the full stop in English, however, you put the letter 'h' (heures) in French – 13.15 therefore becomes 13h15.

Did you know?

The 24-hour clock is used much more in France than it is in England. It is always used in train, bus, ferry and plane timetables. It is also used where we would add 'a.m.' or 'p.m.' to ordinary clock times, such as for doctors' or dentists' appointments, television and radio programmes and shop opening and closing times.

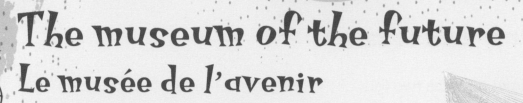

The museum of the future
Le musée de l'avenir

Isabella Witherbottom was visiting the museum of the future, where you can see how things will be in a hundred years' time. There was a school which showed how lessons will be taught in the future. The school had lots of different booths for different subjects.

In 'la **géographie**', geography, Isabella pressed a button marked '**tremblement de terre**' and the whole building seemed to shake.

Next in '**l'histoire**', history, she pressed a button marked '**Révolution française**' and she could hear the crowds marching to the Bastille.

In '**l'anglais**', English, she listened to a holograph of Mr Shakespeare, telling her all about how he came to invent the three witches in Macbeth.

Isabella moved on to 'le **français**', French, where she met a Monsieur Molière, who was a famous French scientist of the future. He became popular for his invention – self-cooking croissants that you did not need to put in the oven!

In 'la **physique**', physics, a Monsieur Einstein took her on a virtual tour of the universe, explaining about 'la **relativité**', relativity.

I just won Wimbledon!

She went on to 'la **chimie**', chemistry, 'la **biologie**', biology, 'la **musique**', music. Then in '**les maths**', maths, she placed her hand on a pad and magically knew the answer to any sums that came up on the computer screen, without having to calculate them in her head!

"I wish my school had one of these," thought Isabella. "I'm not too good at maths and wish the answers would just pop into my head!"

Most of all, she enjoyed 'l'**éducation physique**'. This booth was a virtual world where you could play any sport and you always won!

Find the right booth

Imagine you are visiting a museum of the future. Which booth would you go to if you want to enjoy the following?

géographie	biologie	chimie	anglais	éducation physique
physique	français	musique	maths	histoire

1 A display of giant sunflowers. _____

2 A demonstration of how to turn water into lemonade. _____

3 A walk round an Aztec temple. _____

4 Watching a hurricane travel across the world. _____

5 Scoring a winning goal for France in the European cup. _____

6 Watching Shakespeare direct a play. _____

7 Seeing sums calculate themselves. _____

Top Tips

It is easy to remember the genders of these school subjects. They are all feminine, apart from the languages, 'anglais' and 'français'. 'Maths' is plural, just like in English.

Did you know?

In parts of France, some children live so far from their schools that they have to stay there from Monday to Friday. They sleep in dormitories with their friends. The schools provide all their meals. A time is set aside for doing 'homework', but they also have some time to be sociable. Many French children enjoy this experience.

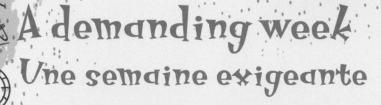

A demanding week
Une semaine exigeante

"Look what I found in the back of the cupboard in the study, whilst I was having a spring clean," said Max, the butler, one day. "It must have belonged to the boy who lived in this house before us."

He handed the piece of paper to Isabella Witherbottom.

"It's a timetable," said Isabella.

	lundi	mardi	mercredi	jeudi	vendredi	samedi
8h00	maths	anglais	_____	français	géographie	histoire
9h00	chimie	physique	_____	biologie	éducation physique	géographie
10h00	récréation	récréation	_____	récréation	récréation	récréation
10h30	anglais	maths		éducation physique	anglais	français
11h30	français	français	_____	maths	maths	maths
12h30	déjeuner	déjeuner		déjeuner	déjeuner	_____
14h30	éducation physique	chimie		anglais	français	_____
15h30	récréation	récréation	_____	récréation	récréation	_____
16h00	biologie	histoire	_____	physique	musique	
17h00	FIN DES COURS					

"Look, school started at eight every morning," said Max. "Then the child had a break at ten. Lunch was from half past twelve until half past two and then there was another break at three thirty."

"School didn't finish until five o'clock!" exclaimed Isabella.

"At least he didn't have school on Wednesdays," pointed out Max.

"So he had maths, chemistry, English, French, P.E. and biology on Mondays," continued Isabella.

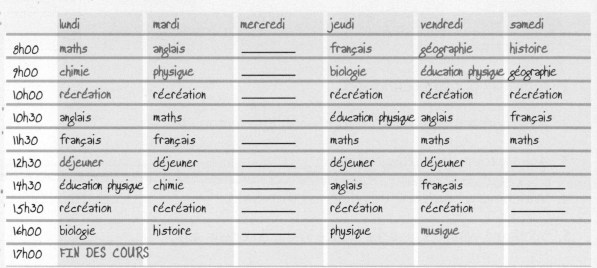

Mercredi! Bliss! No school today.

"His first physics lesson was on Tuesdays," said Max. "And he finished the day with history."

"He had biology on Mondays and Thursdays," said Isabella. "He had geography and music, my two favourite lessons, on Fridays."

"Then he finished on Saturday mornings with maths!" said Max, the butler.

"What! School on Saturday?" exclaimed a shocked Isabella!

Faded labels

The labels on these exercise books have faded and some of the letters have disappeared altogether. Work out which subject each book is used for.

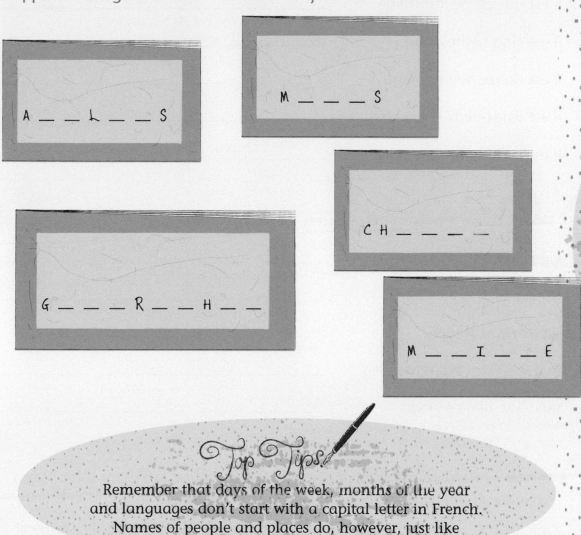

A _ _ L _ _ S

M _ _ _ _ S

CH _ _ _ _ _

G _ _ _ R _ _ H _ _

M _ _ I _ _ E

Top Tips!
Remember that days of the week, months of the year
and languages don't start with a capital letter in French.
Names of people and places do, however, just like
in English.

Did you know?

School in France generally begins at eight and finishes about five. After school, pupils aged seven and above are expected to do homework. They do, however, get really long summer holidays – from the end of June until September. They have holidays at Christmas and Easter, and a week in February. There are also many bank holidays in France.

Revise Time

1 Write these times in the correct order, starting with the earliest.

a   Il est quinze heures trente.   _____

b   Il est cinq heures cinq.   _____

c   Il est douze heures vingt.   _____

d   Il est vingt-deux heures dix.   _____

e   Il est une heure cinquante.   _____

2 Write these times out in figures and say whether they are a.m. or p.m.

a   vingt heures dix   _____   _____

b   trois heures vingt-cinq   _____   _____

c   sept heures trente   _____   _____

d   douze heures quarante-cinq   _____   _____

e   quatorze heures vingt   _____   _____

3 Write out these school subjects in French. The answers have been provided, but the letters have been jumbled up.

michie	queshypi ducétanoi	quemisu	reshoiti	ransiçaf

a   History   _____

b   Chemistry   _____

c   Music   _____

d   French   _____

e   P.E.   _____

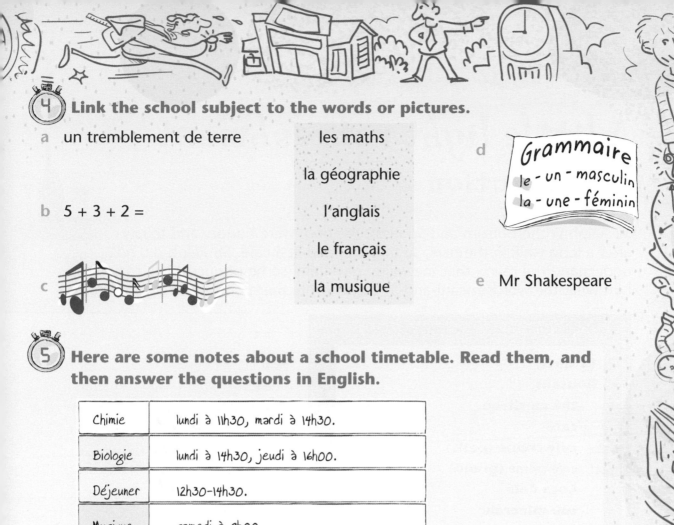

4 **Link the school subject to the words or pictures.**

a   un tremblement de terre

b   5 + 3 + 2 =

c   [musical notes]

les maths

la géographie

l'anglais

le français

la musique

d   *Grammaire*
    le - un - masculin
    la - une - féminin

e   Mr Shakespeare

5 **Here are some notes about a school timetable. Read them, and then answer the questions in English.**

Chimie	lundi à 11h30, mardi à 14h30.
Biologie	lundi à 14h30, jeudi à 16h00.
Déjeuner	12h30-14h30.
Musique	samedi à 9h00.
Anglais	lundi à 10h00, mardi à 11h30, jeudi à 14h30.

a   What time is lunch? _____

b   How many English lessons does he have? _____

c   What time is his chemistry lesson on Tuesday? _____

d   On which days does he have biology? _____

e   Which subject does he only have once a week? _____

6 **The names of the days of the week on which French children go to school have been hidden in this ruler. Find them and then write them out in the correct order.**

L U N D I J E U D I M A R D I S A M E D I V E N D R E D I

_____

A little light refreshment
Une collation

Sir Ralph Witherbottom and Spotless, the dog, were hungry and thirsty after a long walk in the park, so they stopped at a café. Sir Ralph did not understand the menu that the waiter gave him, so he phoned Max. Max told him what the words meant and Sir Ralph wrote them on his paper serviette.

La carte
Boissons

thé au citron	2.50	lemon tea
café	1.50	coffee
café crème (petit)	2.00	white coffee (small)
café crème **(grand)**	3.70	white coffee (large)
Coca-Cola	3.50	Coca-Cola
eau minérale	3.25	mineral water
limonade	2.75	lemonade
vin rouge (verre)	3.50	red wine (glass)
vin blanc (verre)	3.50	white wine (glass)
bière blonde (1/3 l.)	2.75	lager (1/3 of a litre)

Petits plats — Light dishes

sandwich au jambon	5.00	ham sandwich
sandwich au **fromage**	5.00	cheese sandwich
sandwich au **thon**	6.00	tuna sandwich
omelette nature	6.50	plain omelette
omelette au fromage	7.50	cheese omelette
omelette **aux champignons**	7.50	mushroom omelette
salade niçoise	12.50	salad with tuna, anchovies, hard boiled egg
croque-monsieur	8.50	toasted cheese and ham sandwich
croque-madame	9.00	toasted cheese and ham sandwich, with fried egg
gâteaux	3.00 – 4.50	cakes

Menu
Drinks

"Un croque-monsieur et une bière blonde, s'il vous plaît," said Sir Ralph to the waiter.

Spotless barked. "Oh, and a bowl of water and 'un sandwich au jambon' for my trusty friend here!"

Snacks and drinks crossword

Write the French for these words in the puzzle grid.

Verticalement:
1 Sandwich
4 Salad

Horizontalement:
2 Lemon tea
3 Lemonade
5 Glass

Actually, I rather fancied a 'salade niçoise' and 'limonade' today!

Top Tips

Use shortcuts when ordering drinks. 'Un grand crème' is a large white coffee and 'un petit crème' a small one. 'Une limo' is a lemonade and 'un coca' is a coke.

Did you know?

French restaurants have very strict laws. They must include any service charges in the menu price. You can see how much this is by looking for the words 'service compris'. They must always display the menu outside and they must also let you use their toilet, even if you haven't used the restaurant.

Money doesn't grow on trees
L'argent ne tombe pas du ciel

Isabella was counting her money. She had a ten euro note, a five euro note, three one euro coins, a two euro coin, five 50 cent coins, three 20 cent coins, one ten cent coin, five two cent coins and ten one cent coins.

"Max," she said. "How much is all this worth?"

"23 euros 40 cents," said Max.

"That's not enough, as I've got to buy loads of birthday presents this month," said Isabella. "Dad, can I have next month's allowance a little early?"

"I'll have to go to the bank first," said Sir Ralph. "Money doesn't grow on trees, you know."

"Indeed, as the French would say, **'l'argent ne tombe pas du ciel'** – money doesn't fall from the sky," added Max.

"No, it just comes out of the cash machine," laughed Isabella.

"If I were you," said Max, "I'd keep one of those one euro coins back. You need them for the bus. Remember to ask for **'pièces'** for coins and **'billets'** for notes at the bank. You should look at what the **'cours'** is. That's the exchange rate.

"Remember, prices are written down like this.

€5.40

"That strange sign that looks a bit like a capital 'E' is the euro sign. An item with this price on it would cost five euros and 40 cents, for example," explained Max.

I thought 'l'argent ne tombe pas du ciel'.

What can you buy?

Tick which items you can buy with the money in the purse.

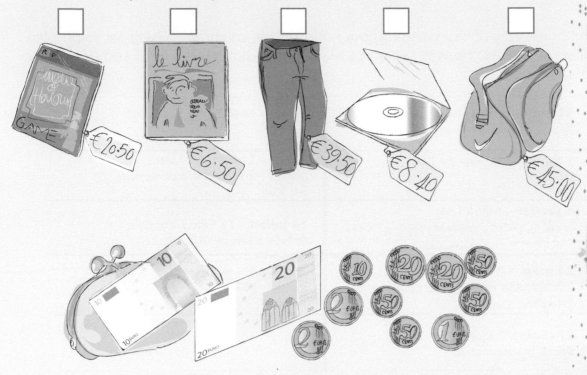

€20·50   €6·50   €39·50   €8·40   €45·00

How would you actually choose to spend the money?

The number of euros you can get for a pound
changes daily and even hourly. You can find out
the exchange rate at any bank, on the Internet or
on the TV.

Did you know?

Many European countries now use the euro as their currency. The notes are
the same everywhere. Each country, however, designed one side of the coins
that they manufactured, so, as the coins can also be used in any of the euro
countries, you may find a French designed coin in, say, Germany.

Let's celebrate
Il faut fêter ça

The housekeeper had written some notes on the calendar to help Sir Ralph plan for some parties. He was talking to Max about what special food and drink they need to order.

31 décembre – La Veille du Nouvel An Réveillon – dinde et champagne	**1 mai** – La **Fête** du Travail muguet
1 janvier – Le Jour de l'An	**8 mai** – La Fête des Mères envoyer des fleurs pour la mère de Sir Ralph
8 février – Mardi Gras crêpes, défilé, costume pour Isabella	**14 juillet** – La Fête Nationale – défilés et feux d'artifice
24 mars – Pâques acheter des œufs en chocolat pour Isabella	**20 juillet** – anniversaire d'Isabella – bougies, gâteau, cadeaux
27 mars – Pâques allez à la grande messe	

"So we'll need turkey and champagne for the late meal on New Year's Eve, on December 31st," said Max. "We can have a rest on New Year's Day after that late night!"

"Then there'll be a costume to buy for Isabella, for the parade on Pancake Day," said Sir Ralph. "I expect she'll want to dress up as her favourite pop star or something. Oh, and we must make sure we've got enough eggs and milk, as well.

"We must buy the chocolate eggs for Easter," suggested Sir Ralph.

"We mustn't forget to get some 'lily of the valley' flowers to give everyone for luck on May 1st, as it's Labour Day and 'muguet' means 'lily of the valley'" said Max.

Fleurs, champagne, feux d'artifice, cadeaux … better start saving now!

"I must remember to send my mother some flowers on Mother's Day," said Sir Ralph.

"We could buy a few fireworks for the National Bank Holiday," said Max.

"We'll need candles for the cake and presents for Miss Isabella's birthday. Let's write the date in the calendar just to make sure we don't forget!" said Max.

Festival search

Find the French words to do with festivals in this word search. The English words have been listed below.

| present | chocolate egg | pancakes | easter | champagne | turkey |

c	r	ê	p	e	s	a	n	c	g	z	e	s	b
y	a	f	e	t	t	r	e	a	o	r	l	s	g
d	a	s	i	n	b	l	e	d	n	w	t	e	v
i	e	t	p	o	û	e	b	e	h	c	h	u	b
n	o	c	s	ë	a	t	d	a	e	b	m	q	o
d	g	r	i	h	h	t	l	u	m	n	m	â	t
e	n	e	n	g	a	p	m	a	h	c	t	p	c
o	e	u	f	e	n	c	h	o	c	o	l	a	t

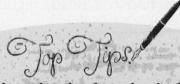

Top Tips

Notice that plurals of words which end in 'eau' add an 'x', not an 's', so 'cadeau' becomes 'cadeaux', presents, and 'gâteau' becomes 'gâteaux', cakes.

Did you know?

The French are very fond of using sugared almonds for celebrations. They give white ones to the guests at weddings. When a baby girl is born or christened, they give pink ones to all their friends and relations, blue ones if it's a baby boy.

Revise Time

1 **Unscramble these names of drinks you could buy in a French café.**

a d e m n a i l o _____

b m è r c e f a c é _____

c i n o v g u e r _____

d t i c é n o t h a u r _____

e r e d l o e b b i n è _____

2 **Answer the following questions.**

a What is a 'croque-monsieur'?

_____

b What do you add to it to make a 'croque-madame'?

_____

c What does the word 'nature' mean in 'omelette nature'?

_____

d Name two ingredients you would find in a 'salade niçoise'.

_____

e What is a cheese sandwich called in French?

_____

3 **Write these prices out, as they would appear on labels.**

a Two euros 50 cents _____

b Five euros 75 cents _____

c 39 euros 25 cents _____

d 65 euros 10 cents _____

e Ten euros _____

18

4 Fill in the 'bank slip' to show all the notes and coins shown here.
Then add up how much there is altogether.

Billets	No	Somme	Pièces	No	Somme
100 euros	_____	_____	2 euros	_____	_____
50 euros	_____	_____	1 euro	_____	_____
20 euros	_____	_____	50 cents	_____	_____
10 euros	_____	_____	20 cents	_____	_____
5 euros	_____	_____	10 cents	_____	_____
			5 cents	_____	_____
			2 cents	_____	_____
			1 cent	_____	_____
Somme	_____				

5 Fill in the missing letter in each word to do with festivals celebrated
in France. What word do these letters form if you string the missing
letters together?

a C __ êpe

b Défil __

c Tra __ ail

d Pâqu __ s

e Ju __ llet

f F __ eurs

g Le Jour du Nouve __ An

h B __ ugie

i An __ iversaire

These letters form the festival: _____

6 Which description goes with which festival? Draw a line to
connect them.

a You have to give people a lily of the valley.

b There are carnival processions on this day.

c There are firework displays.

d You go to a big church service.

e You give flowers on this day.

1 La Fête des Mères

2 La Fête du Travail

3 Mardi Gras

4 Pâques

5 La Fête Nationale

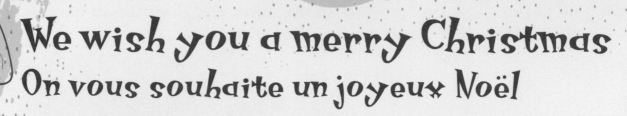

We wish you a merry Christmas
On vous souhaite un joyeux Noël

Isabella had finished writing her Christmas cards which were printed with the words, 'On vous souhaite un joyeux Noël et une bonne année'.

"So we're wishing everybody a merry Christmas and a happy New Year," she said to Max.

"Shall we look at the housekeeper's list, so we can help with the Christmas preparations?" asked Max. "What do we have here? Ah, I see…

le sapin de Noël	"There's the Christmas tree,
la bûche de Noël	the Yule Log, (that's chocolate, you know!),
la crèche	the Christmas nativity scene,
lettre au Père Noël	a letter to Father Christmas,
s'il neige – bonhomme de neige dans le jardin	and, if it snows, making a snowman in the garden.
téléphoner au boulanger – commander la galette des rois	Someone needs to phone the baker to order the '**galette des rois**' – that's the cake the French eat on January 6th."

"Let's do your letter to Father Christmas first," suggested Max.

Cher Père Noël,

Je voudrais bien un ordinateur et un pull rouge.

Merci

Izzy

Hmm, Cher Père Noël – Je voudrais un gros os de Noël.

"A computer and a red jumper," noted Max. "Now, why don't you go and build that snowman, whilst I call the baker?"

Some children came up the garden path, whilst Izzy was rolling a big snowball. They were singing, 'Il est né, le divin enfant.'

Max came outside to listen. "That's my favourite Christmas carol – 'He is born the holy child.' Anyway, better get on, as there's still lots to do!"

Christmas wordsearch

Find these Christmas words hidden in the wordsearch. Some are separated.

galette des rois   sapin   bonhomme de neige   bûche
crèche   père noël   lettre

m	n	o	p	q	r	s	t	e	b
q	a	l	e	t	t	r	e	e	o
s	a	p	i	n	b	l	e	t	n
d	e	s	p	o	û	e	b	t	h
r	o	i	s	ë	c	t	d	e	o
f	g	h	i	l	h	t	l	l	m
c	r	è	c	h	e	r	r	a	m
p	è	r	e	f	n	e	i	g	e

Top Tips

The **pronoun** 'on' really means 'one'.
The French also use it to mean 'we',
'you' and 'they'.

Did you know?

On January 6th, French families buy their 'galette des rois' from the bakery.
This is sliced very carefully, for somewhere hidden in it is a small figure.
Whoever gets that slice becomes King or Queen and chooses a partner for
the day. They wear the two party hats which are supplied with the cake.

Oh what big ears you have!
Comme tu as de grandes oreilles!

Isabella was going to take part in the local play with some friends. They were putting on a performance of 'Le Petit Chaperon Rouge' – Little Red Riding Hood – and she had the main part. Max was kindly helping her with her lines.

"Oh, **grand-mère**, comme tu as de grands **yeux**!" said Isabella. "Ah!" thought Max, "what big eyes you have! All the better to see you.

"C'est pour mieux te **voir**," said Max.

"Oh, grand-mère, comme tu as de grandes **oreilles**!" said Isabella, pointing to her ears.

"C'est pour mieux t'**entendre**," said Max, putting his hands behind his ears.

"Oh, grand-mère, comme tu as une grosse **tête**!" said Isabella, tapping her head.

"C'est pour mieux **penser à toi**," said Max.

"I think that means 'all the better to think of you'," thought Isabella.

"Oh, grand-mère, comme tu as les **jambes** longues!" said Isabella, pointing to her legs.

"C'est pour mieux te **chasser**," said Max, getting ready to chase Isabella.

"Oh, grand-mère, comme tu as les **bras** longs!" said Isabella, stretching out her arms.

"C'est pour mieux t'**attraper**," said Max, stretching his arms out wider to catch Isabella.

"Oh, grand-mère, comme tu as une grande **bouche**!" said Isabella, opening her mouth wide.

"C'est pour mieux te **manger**," said Max, gnashing his teeth.

Max growled. Isabella screamed!

"Very good!" said Max. "Très bien!"

La grande bouche? C'est pour te mieux manger!

The monster

Read this description of a monster. Draw it in the box provided.

Il a deux grandes têtes, cinq oreilles, six yeux, deux grandes bouches, six jambes longues, et huit bras longs.

Top Tips

In French you often use 'le', 'la' or 'les' instead of 'un', 'une' or 'des' for parts of the body, so you say 'the' instead of 'a', 'an' or 'some'. For example, 'je me brosse les dents' means 'I brush my teeth'.

Did you know?

'Chaperon' – riding hood – is also the French word for 'chaperone'. A chaperone is a person who protects you. When children take part in a professional theatre production, the chaperone sits backstage with them to look after them. Poor Red Riding Hood, however, had only her hooded cloak for protection when she went into the forest to visit her grandmother.

Fitness training
Se mettre en forme

Sir Ralph wanted to get fit, so he invented a machine on which he could practise lots of different sports. Max was helping him to label all the buttons in French, so that Sir Ralph could sell his invention to local gyms.

Sir Ralph showed Max each of the functions and Max wrote the labels. First Sir Ralph demonstrated jogging.

Max wrote, '**faire du jogging**'.

Next, the machine was pulling his arms out and making him jump up into the air. Max wrote, 'faire du **keepfit**'.

Then, Sir Ralph was holding a tennis racket and hitting a tennis ball against the wall onto which the machine had projected a picture of a tennis court. Max wrote, '**jouer au tennis**'.

After that, Sir Ralph was playing squash, then golf and then football. Max wrote, 'jouer au **squash**, jouer au **golf**, jouer au **football**'. Then he was swimming, horse riding, and doing gymnastics. Max wrote 'faire de la **natation**, faire de l'**équitation** and 'faire de la **gymnastique**'.

Sir Ralph was now getting a little tired, but still managed to practise athletics and skiing on the machine. Max wrote 'faire de l'**athlétisme**' and 'faire du **ski**'.

By this time, poor Sir Ralph was so out of breath he could hardly speak. He panted, "I think this is going to be one of my best selling inventions, Max, but I think I may have slightly overdone it!" – and with that he collapsed in a heap on the floor!

Faire du keepfit, du jogging, jouer au tennis, au golf …

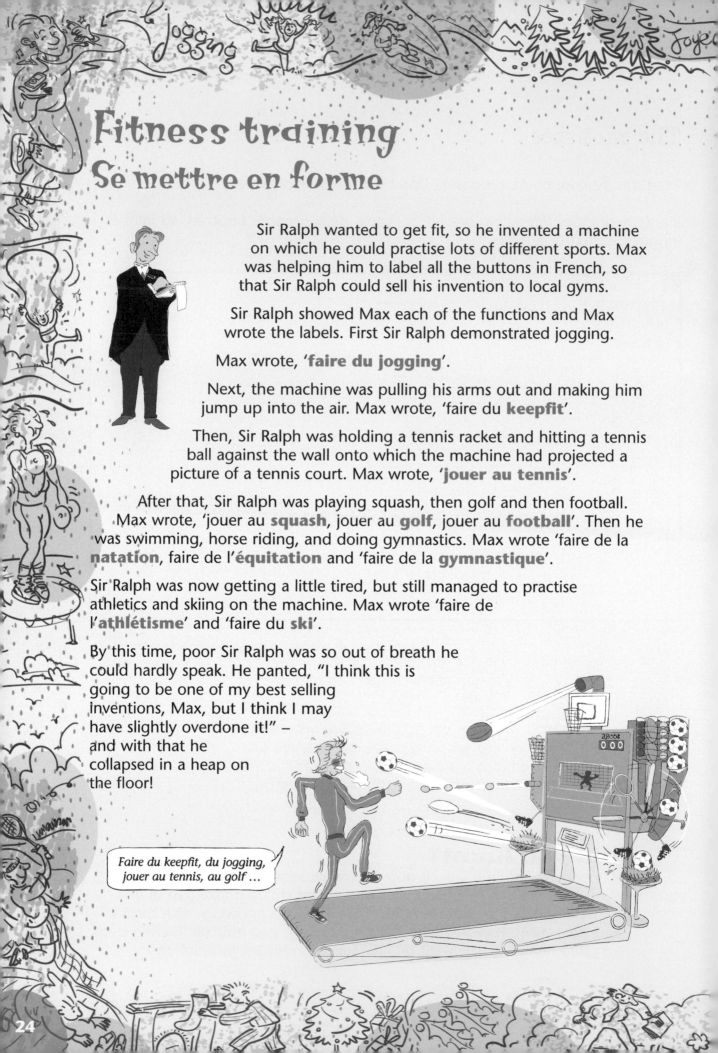

24

Sports wordsearch

Find these words to do with sports in the wordsearch.

tennis

centre sportif

athlétisme

jogging

natation

équitation

squash

ski

gymnastique

a	v	f	b	e	k	n	t	h	z	e	q	j	m
d	o	r	w	t	e	n	n	i	s	r	s	t	u
c	e	n	t	r	e	v	w	x	p	f	f	g	g
b	é	q	u	i	t	a	t	i	o	n	f	g	a
g	h	g	h	h	f	i	i	j	r	j	k	k	t
l	j	o	g	g	i	n	g	l	t	q	q	r	h
n	o	l	s	s	t	a	a	p	i	l	q	r	l
r	é	f	s	t	n	t	i	t	f	g	u	v	é
s	q	u	a	s	h	a	w	w	x	y	b	t	t
y	u	z	z	a	n	t	a	a	u	b	b	c	i
c	i	c	d	d	l	i	e	s	f	f	s	o	s
f	t	g	g	t	h	o	i	d	k	k	l	l	m
l	a	j	g	y	m	n	a	s	t	i	q	u	e
j	t	j	k	k	l	w	q	v	n	m	y	o	e
w	n	w	r	b	n	w	a	n	f	g	b	x	a

Top Tips

Notice that you 'jouer au' games, but 'faire de la, du' or 'de l'' activities. So it's 'jouer *au* golf', but 'faire *du* ski'.

Did you know?

Sport is important to the French. They regard football as their national sport. The most famous bike race in the world, 'le **Tour de France**', is held every July in France. The French Open Tennis Championships take place just before the British Wimbledon Tennis Championships. Many of the world's winter sports are held in the Alps in France.

Revise Time

1 **Answer the following questions.**

a   What is 'Father Christmas' in French? _____

b   What is the name of the chocolate cake eaten at Christmas time?

_____

c   What is the 'galette des rois'? _____

d   What is 'un bonhomme de neige'? _____

e   How do you say 'Happy New Year' in French?

_____

2 **Look at the English words and expressions. Find the French words, hidden in the streamer and write them out.**

Joyeux Nëel apincrèc ePèr Noëlilestn éledivi enf ntbonneannée

a   Merry Christmas   _____

b   Happy New Year   _____

c   Christmas tree   _____

d   The first line of a French Christmas carol   _____

e   Nativity scene   _____

f   Father Christmas   _____

3 **Join the parts of the body to the activities they might do.**

a   bouche   attraper

b   yeux   manger

c   oreilles   chasser

d   jambes   entendre

e   bras   voir

4 Fill in the missing words in this conversation.

a "Oh, grand-mère, comme tu as de grands _____."

b "C'est pour mieux _____ voir."

c "Oh, grand-mère, comme tu as de _____ oreilles!"

d "C'est pour _____ t'entendre."

e "Oh, grand-mère, comme tu as _____ grosse tête!"

f "C'est pour mieux _____ à toi."

g "Oh, grand-mère, comme tu as les jambes _____!"

h "C'est pour mieux te _____."

5 Here are some sports and activities. Put them in the correct box.

| jogging | keepfit | tennis | squash | golf | football |
| natation | équitation | | gymnastique | ski | |

faire de la/de l'	faire du	jouer au

6 Fill in the missing letters in these sporting activities, then string the letters together to spell out another activity.

a Équitatio __

b __ thlétisme

c __ ennis

d Footb __ ll

e Keepfi __

f Sk __

g G __ lf

h Gym __ astique

Other activity = _____

I love it!
Je l'adore

Isabella had been asked to help judge a painting competition, held at the little gallery near where they lived. She was writing down what she thought about the eight shortlisted pictures.

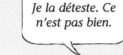

"Oh, I don't like this one at all," she said, looking at the painting numbered one – a picture of an ugly horse. "I don't like that, it's not good!" She wrote, '**Je ne l'aime pas du tout**' next to number one on the form. In brackets she put '**Ce n'est pas bien**'. The second picture was even worse and she hated it, so she wrote, '**Je la déteste**'.

> Je la déteste. Ce n'est pas bien.

The third picture was a little better, but Isabella still did not like it really. She wrote '**Je ne l'aime pas**'.

The fourth picture was of a garden, but Isabella still did not like it all that much, so she wrote, '**Je ne l'aime pas beaucoup**'.

She looked at the one of a country cottage and decided it was all right. She wrote, '**Ça va**' on the form.

"I quite like that," she thought, when she saw picture number six. She noted down, '**Je l'aime bien**'.

"I love picture number seven," she thought. She wrote '**Je l'aime**'.

Picture number eight was of a beautiful beach. "I adore it. It's fantastic, wonderful, superb!" and scribbled enthusiastically, '**Je l'adore**. Elle est **formidable, magnifique, super**!'.

She handed in her form at the exit of the gallery and made her way home, feeling rather pleased that they had asked her her opinion.

Which picture wins?

The pictures in a competition are awarded points according to what the three judges say. This chart shows you how the points are awarded. Which picture gets the most number of points?

Je la déteste: –4 points	Ça va: +1 point
Je ne l'aime pas du tout: –3 points	Je l'aime bien: +2 points
Je ne l'aime pas: –2 points	Je l'aime: +3 points
Je ne l'aime pas beaucoup: –1 point	Je l'adore: +4 points

What the judges say:

"Je ne l'aime pas."	"Je l'adore."	"Ça va."
"Je l'aime bien."	"Je ne l'aime pas du tout."	"Je l'aime bien."
"Ça va."	"Je la déteste."	"Je ne l'aime pas beaucoup."
☐	☐	☐

Top Tips

'Le' means 'him' or 'it' for masculine words. 'La' means 'her', or 'it' for feminine words. They go in front of the verb. If the verb begins with a vowel, you use 'l'.

Did you know?

The verb '**aimer**' means 'to love' or 'to like'. To distinguish between the two, where there might be confusion, you add 'bien' to make it mean 'to like'. If you want to be really clear about how strongly you feel, just say 'j'adore'.

Memory training course
Entrainement pour la mémoire

Sir Ralph bought himself a book – 'A Five Day Course in Memory Improvement'.

"There are some excellent ideas in here for learning new languages," he said to Max. "It says that many words are very similar to the English."

A FIVE DAY COURSE IN MEMORY IMPROVEMENT

"Indeed, sir," said Max. "There are words like '**éléphant**', – elephant, '**carotte**', – carrot, '**octobre**' – October, '**intelligent**' – intelligent, '**violet**', violet, and '**hamster**', hamster."

"It also says," said Sir Ralph "that it helps if the word reminds you of something. I suppose like me thinking of 'huit' as 'wheat' that grows in the field. Oh, and do you remember when I wrote 'an', year, and 'âne' donkey, and got them mixed up? I can remember both words if I think of 'donkey's years'!"

"Then you could remember '**vin**', wine, because you like to have it delivered by the van load and it is, in fact, pronounced 'van'. Of course, you write it 'V I N', so it's a bit like 'vinegar', which is similar to the word for 'bitter wine' – '**vinaigre**'. Then there's '**vert**', like 'verdigris' – the greenish colour that copper goes in the open air."

"It also says," continued Sir Ralph, "that professional actors read their lines out loud twelve times and then they more or less know them."

"So, say new words twelve times when you first come across them," said Max.

"It also recommends collecting interesting words," said Sir Ralph. "I shall have to buy a nice new notebook."

Bouteille, bouteille, bouteille – so that's twelve green bottles — not ten like the song!"

Memory aid

Here are twelve words you might want to learn. Join each one up to the best way of remembering them.

la **petite-fille** – the granddaughter

la chambre – the bedroom

le singe – the monkey

le **cousin** – the cousin

Words which sound like English

la **poubelle** – the dustbin (n.b. '**pouer**' means to smell and '**belle**' means beautiful)

le **neveu** – the nephew

grand – big, tall

Words which remind you of something

Words for saying out loud twelve times

la **girafe** – the giraffe

la **bouche** – the mouth

le **gratte-ciel** – the skyscraper (n.b. '**gratter**' means to scratch and '**ciel**' means sky)

Words to add to your collection

la **salle de bains** – the bathroom (literally 'the hall of the baths')

le **bébé** – the baby

Top Tips

Try to collect a few new words each week. Find a notebook to write them in and don't forget to say them out loud 12 times.

Did you know?

When you learn a new language, you learn to recognise words when you hear and see them, a long time before you can actually use those words in speech or writing, without having to look them up. You can make rapid progress if you turn some of the words and phrases you recognise into ones you use yourself.

A secret is discovered
On découvre un secret

Isabella had found a piece of old crumpled paper under her bed, when looking for a missing shoe. She smoothed it out and saw it had writing on it.

Allez dans le jardin. De la cuisine, deux pas au nord, cinq pas à l'est. Trouvez les pièces dans la terre, sous le grand sapin. Utilisez les mains pour creuser. Le trésor est délicat. Le trésor, c'est magnifique!

"This looks like a treasure hunt," said Isabella. "Some words are quite easy. 'Allez' – that means 'go'. I've got to go somewhere.

"'De la cuisine' – 'from the 'kitchen'.

"'Deux'? That's a number – 'un, deux, trois, quatre, cinq' – one, two, three, four, five.

"'Pièces?' Pieces? Ah yes – 'une pièce d'un euro' – that's a one euro coin, so 'pièces' must be 'coins'.

"'Terre'? I know that, because 'tremblement de terre' is an earthquake, so 'terre' means earth.

"'Sous le grand sapin'? Well, 'grand' is big and 'sapin' is the tree we put up at Christmas. Of course! The tall pine tree! There are two pine trees in the garden though. Ah! So 'jardin' means 'garden'. It's the tree that's two ... two paces north and five paces east!

"'Utilisez'? ... utilise, or use ... the 'mains' ... hands .... In order to '**creuser**' ... what could this mean? Use your hands to ... I know – to dig! Come on, Spotless – this sounds right up your street!"

'Utilisez les mains pour creuser.' Use your hands to dig – paws do the trick much better!

Read the note

You arrive at your holiday home in France to find a note on the table. Work out what it says.

Regardez la vidéo du Tour de France et des sports d'hiver dans les Alpes. C'est super! Allez dans la cuisine. Il y a une bouteille de vin, du Coca Cola, des verres et des gâteaux sur la table.

_____

_____

_____

_____

_____

_____

_____

_____

Top Tips

Read new French texts through three times, jotting down words you understand in pencil as you go along. You will be astonished at how much more you understand the third time.

Did you know?

Reading in French is a little different. First, you see what the text is – a note from the window cleaner, perhaps. Then you fill in the words you recognise. Next, you fill in the words you can work out, because maybe they are similar in English. You will be left with a few gaps, but may be able to work out the sense of the note. Occasionally, however, you will have to look those words up in a dictionary. It is a bit like doing a jigsaw puzzle.

Revise Time

1 Answer these questions.

a You see a lovely jumper in the shop. What do you say?

1 ☐ Ça va.   2 ☐ Je ne l'aime pas beaucoup.   3 ☐ Je l'aime.

b Your brother is watching a horrid television programme. What do you say?

1 ☐ Je ne l'aime pas du tout.   2 ☐ Je l'aime.   3 ☐ Je l'adore.

c You see a cute puppy. What do you say?

1 ☐ Je le déteste.   2 ☐ Je ne l'aime pas.   3 ☐ Je l'adore.

d You hear a fantastic CD. What do you say?

1 ☐ Ça va.   2 ☐ Je ne l'aime pas.   3 ☐ C'est super.

2 Write the French for the following.

a I love it. _____

b I hate it. _____

c I don't like it at all. _____

d I quite like it. _____

e It's not very good. _____

3 Link up the words with the possible way of remembering them.

a Mort-aux-rats (f) – Rat poison (literally: death to the rats)   Remember it is similar to English.

b Magnifique – Magnificent   Say it twelve times.

c Sapin (m) de Noël – Christmas tree   Add it to my collection.

d Bouche (f) – Mouth   Remember it is similar to English.

e Jouer au rugby – Play rugby   Say it twelve times.

4 How well do you know these words and expressions?

Write the English for:

a jardin _____

b cuisine _____

c nord _____

Write the French for:

d two _____

e arms _____

f pine tree _____

5 This note was stuck to a fridge. Read it three times, then answer the question and follow the instructions to help you to work out what it means.

> Sur la table, il y a une bouteille de limonade, des verres, et des sandwichs au fromage pour vous. Il y a un match de football à la télé à 15h30. Dans la cave, il y a une bouteille de vin rouge pour Papa. Je vais chez boulanger pour commander la galette des rois.
>
> À bientôt, Maman.

a What type of note do you think this is? Who might have left it there and why?

_____

b Underline the words you recognise, and write in what they mean over the top.

c Try to guess what some of the other words mean and write these in as well.

d There may still be a few words you do not understand, but they may be in the glossary.

6 Now answer these questions about the note on the fridge.

a Where is the lemonade? _____

b What can you eat? _____

c What is happening at half past three? _____

d What is in the cellar for Dad? _____

e Where has Mum gone? _____

A surprise in the cellar
Une surprise dans la cave

Isabella found a note, which had been pushed under the front door.

> Chère famille Witherbottom,
>
> Dans la cave, derrière l'étagère avec les vingt bouteilles de **cidre**, il y a un grand **carton** rouge. Dans le carton, il y a deux bouteilles de bière blonde pour Monsieur Witherbottom et une bouteille de limonade pour Mademoiselle Izzy. Il y a aussi les tickets pour le club de tennis. Le club de tennis, c'est **formidable**.
>
> Bonne journée.
>
> Famille Lyon

"I understand most of it," she said to Max. "'Dans la cave' – in the cellar – but what's 'derrière'?"

Max cleared his throat and patted his bottom.

"Oh, behind!" giggled Isabella when she understood what Max meant. "Behind the 'étagère', shelves, 'avec les vingt bouteilles de' – with twenty bottles of … 'cidre'?"

"'Cider'?" suggested Max.

'Ticket', 'club', 'carton', 'tennis'. Are we talking French or English here?!

"There's a big red … 'carton' – oh, cardboard box, I suppose. There are … two bottles of lager – bière blonde – for … Mr Witherbottom …. and … a bottle of lemonade for me! Then tickets for the tennis 'club' – that's an easy word. There are so many words which are similar to English! The tennis club is 'formidable'. I know that one … fantastic. 'Bonne journée' – have a nice day. Oh, the Lyon family lived here before we moved in – how lovely, they left us a present. Formidable!"

Wheel of fortune

Find the French words, which are the same as English hidden in this wheel.

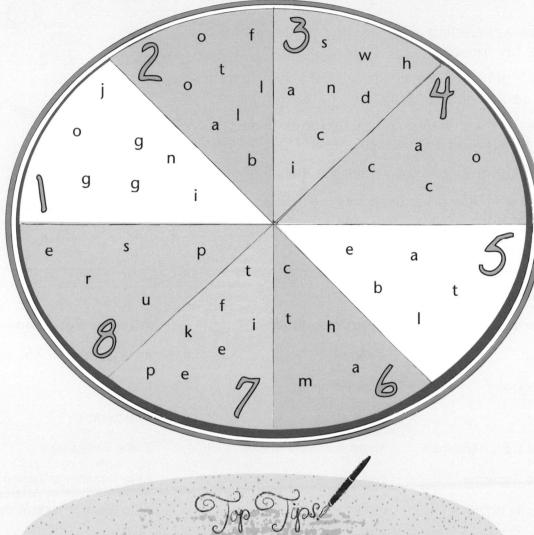

Top Tips!

You will often understand a text after reading it three times. Suddenly a word you did not understand may sound much more like the English, especially if you say it out loud.

Did you know?

An organisation called the 'Académie française' tries to stop foreign words being used by French-speaking people and encourages people to use a French expression where they can. They have obviously not always been successful and it can be quite confusing sometimes. For instance, some French people say 'le weekend' and others say 'la fin de semaine' – the end of the week.

What a surprise!
Quelle surprise!

Il faut faire du keepfit. I'd rather 'manger une glace'.

Isabella was reading an email she had just got from one of her friends.

"I don't get this," she said to Max. "'Je fais du karaté depuis deux ans.' I know it's something to do with karate."

"It means she's been doing karate for two years, but word for word it says 'I do karate since two years'."

"It's so complicated," complained Isabella.

"There are a few other expressions which are completely different from English," said Max.

Max typed a few more for Isabella.

French	Direct translation	What we say in English
Il faut	It needs	It is necessary to/you must
Il fait noir	It makes black	It is dark
Il y a	It there has	There is/are
Il y a trois semaines	There are three weeks	Three weeks ago
Chez Suzanne	(We actually have no word at	At/to Suzanne's (home)
Chez le boucher	all like 'chez')	At/to the butcher's (shop)
Ça m'est égal	That's equal to me	I don't mind
Tout d'un coup	All of a blow	Suddenly

"Argh!" said Isabella.

"Don't worry," said Max. "It's not all bad news. Remember all those English words they use, such as 'football', 'keepfit', 'violet'. Also, French word order is more often than not exactly the same as English, for example 'Je mange une glace' word for word means, 'I eat an ice-cream'."

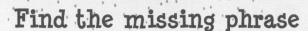

Find the missing phrase

Fill in the missing letter in each phrase. Then string all the missing letters together to spell out a French phrase that means 'it's necessary to go back'.

1 _ l y a trois semaines

2 I _ y a

3 Il _ ait noir

4 Ça m'est ég _ l

5 Dep _ is deux semaines

6 _ out d'un coup

7 Il y a t _ ois semaines

8 Ch _ z Marc

9 Tout d'u _ coup

10 Il fai _ noir

11 Chez le bouche _

12 Il y a d _ ux semaines

13 Je fais du ka _ até

Other phrase: _____

Words and phrases you can not translate directly to or from another language are called idioms. Learn a few of these French idioms off by heart – you will sound like a real French person!

Did you know?

If we find something odd in the way the French say something, French people learning English will find what we do strange as well. To them 'I have been doing karate for two years' sounds as if you're not doing it any more. 'Je fais du karaté depuis deux ans' – 'I do karate since two years' – clearly means you are still doing it.

Skeletons and jelly
Les squelettes et la gelée

door – porte

paint – peindre

kitchen – cuisine

repair – réparer

window – fenêtre

broken – cassé

lounge – salon

change – changer

curtain – rideau

lamp – lampe

Sir Ralph made a list for the man who was going to do some repair work for them. He looked up all the words he needed in a dictionary. He showed Max the list.

Peignez les rideaux? Cassez la lampe?

"Oh dear," said Max. "How will he know what he has to repair, what he has to paint and where all these items are? If you only use words, your language is like a lump of jelly – it's got no form. You need to build the skeleton, giving it a backbone – it's called grammar!"

Sir Ralph's face fell.

"You just need to put the **verbs** into action," said Max, writing out another note. "So it's, 'Peignez la porte, réparez la fenêtre cassée, changez la lampe et les rideaux.' Of course, I've also put in the correct word for 'the' and made 'cassé' **feminine** by adding an 'e' to **agree** with 'fenêtre'. Then you must use a **preposition** to show where all of these things are, like, 'la porte dans la cuisine', for example."

Sir Ralph started to rewrite the note, just like Max had explained – in sentences!

"And don't forget to say please!" reminded Max.

Peignez la porte dans la cuisine, réparez la fenêtre cassée dans le salon, et changez la lampe et les rideaux dans le salon s'il vous plaît.

A note to the workman

Put all these words together to make a sensible note to someone who is going to do some work around the house. There is only one version which will be truly correct!

Peignez	Peignez	Réparez	le
verte	cassée	salon	
salle à manger	lampe	bleu	
dans	la	la	
salle à manger		la	

_____

_____

_____

_____

Top Tips

Most French textbooks and French-English dictionaries have grammar notes in them. Some grammar points are included in the back of this book in the glossary.

Did you know?

Grammar helps to make what you write or say clear. For example, using verbs correctly can show us which person is doing which action and whether they are doing it in the past, present or future. Also you need to remember to use 'le' (**masculine**) or 'la' (feminine) before nouns to mean 'the', and to alter the spelling of any **adjectives** to masculine, feminine and **plural** as well.

Revise Time

1 **Read this letter and underline all of the words which are the same or similar in English.**

lundi, 5 novembre

Salut!

Ce soir je vais faire du jogging et du keepfit. À sept heures, je vais regarder le match d'hockey à la télé. Demain, je vais écrire ma lettre au Père Noël. Je voudrais un pull bleu et un serpent.

À bientôt,

Luc

2 **Write the French for these words.**

a Music   _____

b Sandwich   _____

c Football   _____

d Skiing   _____

e Superb   _____

3 **Choose the right idiom. Match up the phrase with the situation.**

a You need to do something.   Il y a trois semaines …

b Something happens suddenly.   Il faut …

c You are going to Luc's house.   Chez Luc

d You are going to the baker's.   Tout d'un coup

e You did something three weeks ago.   Chez le boulanger

4 Unscramble these idioms.

a h e c z   _____

b san xude puised _____

c aç 'mset élag   _____

d y li a   _____

e strio san li a y _____

5 Write out the following words in French.

a Paint   _____

b Change   _____

c Repair   _____

d In   _____

e Broken (when you're talking about a chair – hint, chair is feminine in French)

_____

6 Underline the French word which means the same as the English one.

a To paint
   peindre   peignez   réparez

b Blue (when talking about the dining room, which is feminine)
   bleu   verte   bleue

c Repair (when you are giving someone an instruction)
   changez   réparer   réparez

d The (when talking about the lounge, which is masculine)
   les   le   la

e In
   en   chez   dans

Glossary

à about/at/to
adorer to adore, to love
aimer to like, to love
aimer bien to like
allez go (giving an order)
anglais English
argent (m) money
athlétisme (m) athletics
attraper to catch
au at the/to the/with (masculine)
aux at the/to the/with (plural)

beaucoup a lot, much
bière (f) blonde lager
billet (m) note
biologie (f) biology
blanc white
boisson (f) drink
bonhomme (m) de neige snowman
bouche (f) mouth
boucher (m) butcher
bras (m) arm
bûche (f) de Noël Yule Log a chocolate sponge roll covered in chocolate

ça m'est égal I don't mind
ça va it's alright
café (m) cafe/coffee
café crème white coffee
carotte (f) carrot
carte (f) card/map/ticket
carton (m) cardboard box
ce n'est pas bien it's not good
champignon (m) mushroom
chasser to chase

chez at the home / place of
chimie (f) chemistry
cidre (m) cider
ciel (m) sky/Heaven
cinq five
cinquante fifty
coca-cola (m) coca-cola
cours (m) exchange rate
crèche (f) manger/crib/ nativity scene
creuser to dig
croque-madame (m) toasted cheese and ham sandwich with a fried egg on top
croque-monsieur (m) toasted cheese and ham sandwich
cuisine (f) kitchen

déjeuner (m) lunch
derrière behind
détester to hate
dix ten
dix-neuf nineteen
du from the/of the/some (masculine)
du tout at all

eau (f) minérale mineral water
éducation physique (f) PE (Physical education)
éléphant (m) elephant
entendre to hear
équitation (f) horse riding

faire to do/make
fête (f) saint's day – on this day, you have a celebration in honour of the saint you were named after

fin (f) end
football (m) football
formidable fantastic
français French
fromage (m) cheese

galette (f) des rois special cake eaten on 6th January
gâteau (m) (x for plural) cake
géographie (f) geography
golf (m) golf
grand big, tall
grand-mère (f) grandmother
gratter to scratch
gymnastique (f) gym/P.E.

hamster (m) hamster
heure (f) hour/o'clock
histoire (f) history/story
huit eight

il faut it is necessary
il y a there is, are/ago
intelligent intelligent

jambe (f) leg
jambon (m) ham
jardin (m) garden
je I
jeudi Thursday
jogging (m) jogging
jouer to play

keepfit (m) keep-fit

la the (feminine)
le the (masculine)
les the (plural)
limonade (f) lemonade
lundi Monday

magnifique magnificent
main (f) hand
manger to eat
mardi Tuesday
maths (f pl) maths
mercredi Wednesday
Monsieur Mr/sir
musique (f) music

natation (f) swimming
ne…pas not
noir black/dark
nord (m) north

octobre October
omelette (f) omelette
oreille (f) ear

pas (m) step/pace
penser to think
Père (m) Noël Father Christmas
petit small
physique (f) physics
pièce (f) coin
plat (m) dish, item on menu
pouer to smell bad

quarante forty
quatorze fourteen
quinze fifteen

récréation (f) break
relativité (f) relativity
Révolution (f) française French Revolution
rouge red

salade (f) niçoise salad with anchovies, tuna and hard-boiled eggs
samedi Saturday
sandwich (m) sandwich
sapin (m) fir tree
sapin de Noël Christmas tree

seize sixteen
semaine (f) week
ski (m) skiing
sous beneath
squash (m) squash
super superb

tennis (m) tennis
terre (f) earth
tête (f) head
thé (m) au citron lemon tea
thon (m) tuna
toi you
tomber to fall
Tour (m) de France bike race which takes place each summer in France
tout d'un coup suddenly
treize thirteen
tremblement (m) de terre earthquake
trente thirty
trois three
trouver to find

utilisez use (giving an order)

Veille (f) du Nouvel An New Year's Eve
vendredi Friday
vert green
vin (m) wine
vinaigre sour wine/vinegar
vingt twenty
vingt et un twenty-one
violet violet
voir to see

yeux (pl) eyes

Adjective A describing word. Examples are 'big', 'long', 'red.

Agree To make something agree is to use the correct gender, number, part or tense of an adjective ('il est bleu'), verb ('nous allons') or pronoun ('ton jardin').

Feminine/Masculine All French nouns, not just the ones to do with people, are either masculine or feminine. It is important to know which, so that you can work out the right words for 'the', 'a', 'my', 'his', etc and make adjectives agree.

All the nouns in this glossary are marked with 'f' feminine or 'm' masculine.

Plural More than one.

Preposition Small word which shows where people or things are, or how they are related to each other. Examples are 'in', 'en', 'sous'.

Pronoun Small word used instead of noun. Examples are 'I', 'she', 'he', 'it', 'you'.

Verb A doing word.

Answers

Page 5

1 Il est quinze heures cinq – Five past three in the afternoon
2 Il est neuf heures dix – Ten past nine in the morning
3 Il est vingt heures vingt – Twenty past eight in the evening
4 Il est dix-huit heures trente – 6.30 p.m.
5 Il est treize heures quarante-cinq – Quarter to two in the afternoon

Page 7

1 A display of giant sunflowers – biologie
2 A demonstration of how to turn water into lemonade – chimie
3 A walk round an Aztec temple – histoire
4 Watching a hurricane travel across the world – géographie
5 Scoring a winning goal for France in the European cup – éducation physique
6 Watching Shakespeare direct a play – anglais
7 Seeing sums calculate themselves – maths

Page 9

ANGLAIS, MATHS, CHIMIE, GEOGRAPHIE, MUSIQUE

Pages 10–11 Revision exercises

Exercise 1
a Il est une heure cinquante.
b Il est cinq heures cinq.
c Il est douze heures vingt.
d Il est quinze heures trente.
e Il est vingt-deux heures dix.

Exercise 2
a 20h10 p.m.
b 3h25 a.m.
c 7h30 a.m.
d 12h45 p.m.
e 14h20 p.m.

Exercise 3
a histoire
b chimie
c musique
d français
e éducation physique

Exercise 4
a un tremblement de terre – la géographie
b 5+3+2 – les maths
c musical notes – la musique
d French exercise book – le français
e Mr Shakespeare – l'anglais

Exercise 5
a 12.30 – 14.30 (half past twelve until half past two)
b three
c 14.30 (half past two)
d Monday and Thursday
e music

Exercise 6
lundi, mardi, jeudi, vendredi, samedi

Page 13
1 sandwich
2 thé au citron
3 limonade
4 salade
5 verre

Page 15
You have €37.50, so you can buy the computer game, the book, and the CD.

Page 17

c	r	ê	p	e	s	a	n	c	g	z	e	s	b
y	a	f	e	t	t	r	e	a	o	r	l	s	g
d	a	s	i	n	b	l	e	d	n	w	t	e	v
i	e	t	p	o	u	e	b	e	h	c	h	u	b
n	o	c	s	e	a	t	d	a	e	b	m	q	o
d	g	r	i	h	h	t	l	u	m	n	m	â	t
e	n	e	n	g	a	p	m	a	h	c	t	p	c
o	e	u	f	e	n	c	h	o	c	o	l	a	t

Pages 18–19 Revision exercises

Exercise 1
a limonade
b café crème
c vin rouge
d thé au citron
e bière blonde

Exercise 2
a a toasted ham and cheese sandwich
b a fried egg
c plain
d anchovies, tuna, hard-boiled eggs, salad (any two)
e sandwich au fromage

Exercise 3
a €2.50 b €5.75 c €39.25 d €65.10
e €10.00

Exercise 4

Billets	No	Somme	Pièces	No	Somme
100 euros	–	–	2 euros	1	2
50 euros	–	–	1 euro	3	3
20 euros	1	20	50 cents	5	2.50
10 euros	1	10	20 cents	3	60
5 euros	2	10	10 cents	5	50
			5 cents	–	–
			2 cents	2	4
			1 cent	5	5
Somme	€48.69				48.69

Exercise 5
a Crêpe
b Défilé
c Travail
d Pâques
e Juillet
f Fleurs
g Le Jour du Nouvel An
h Bougie
i Anniversaire

Other festival word = Réveillon

Exercise 6
a 2　**b** 3　**c** 5　**d** 4　**e** 1

Page 21

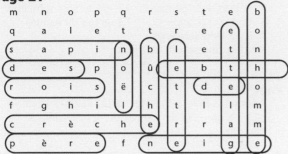

m	n	o	p	q	r	s	t	e		b
q	a	l	e	t	t	r	e	e		o
s	a	p	i	n	b	l	e	t		n
d	e	s	p	o	û	e	b	t		h
r	o	i	s	ë	c	t	d	e		o
f	g	h	i	l	h	t	l	l		m
c	r	è	c	h	e	r	r	a		m
p	è	r	e	f	n	e	i	g		e

Page 23

Your monster should have two big heads, five ears, six eyes, two big mouths, six long legs, and eight long arms.

Page 25

Words you should have found:

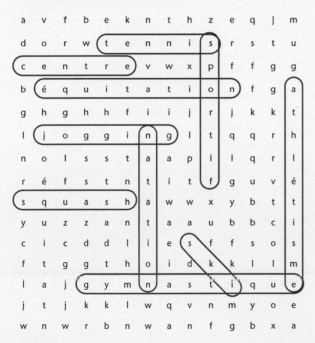

a	v	f	b	e	k	n	t	h	z	e	q	J	m
d	o	r	w	t	e	n	n	i	s	r	s	t	u
c	e	n	t	r	e	v	w	x	p	f	f	g	g
b	é	q	u	i	t	a	t	i	o	n	f	g	a
g	h	g	h	h	f	i	i	j	r	j	k	k	t
l	j	o	g	g	i	n	g	l	t	q	q	r	h
n	o	l	s	s	t	a	a	p	i	l	q	r	l
r	é	f	s	t	n	t	i	t	f	g	u	v	é
s	q	u	a	s	h	a	w	w	x	y	b	t	t
y	u	z	z	a	n	t	a	a	u	b	b	c	i
c	i	c	d	d	l	i	e	s	f	f	s	o	s
f	t	g	g	t	h	o	i	d	k	k	l	l	m
l	a	j	g	y	m	n	a	s	t	i	q	u	e
j	t	j	k	k	l	w	q	v	n	m	y	o	e
w	n	w	r	b	n	w	a	n	f	g	b	x	a

Pages 26–27　Revision exercises

Exercise 1
a Père Noël
b bûche de Noël
c cake eaten January 6th in France
d a snowman
e Bonne Année

Exercise 2
a Merry Christmas – Joyeux Noël
b Happy New Year – Bonne année
c Christmas tree – sapin
d The first line of a French Christmas carol – il est né le divin enfant

e Nativity scene – crèche
f Father Christmas – Père Noël

Exercise 3
a bouche – manger　　**d** jambes – chasser
b yeux – voir　　　　**e** bras – attraper
c oreilles – entendre

Exercise 4
a "Oh, grand-mère, comme tu as de grands yeux."
b "C'est pour mieux te voir."
c "Oh, grand-mère, comme tu as de grandes oreilles!"
d "C'est pour mieux t'entendre."
e "Oh, grand-mère, comme tu as une grosse tête!"
f "C'est pour mieux penser à toi."
g "Oh, grand-mère, comme tu as les jambes longues!"
h "C'est pour mieux te chasser."

Exercise 5
faire de la/de l' – natation, équitation, gymnastique
faire du – jogging, keepfit, ski
jouer au – tennis, squash, golf, football

Exercise 6
a équitation　　　**e** keepfit
b athlétisme　　　**f** ski
c tennis　　　　　**g** golf
d football　　　　**h** gymnastique
Other activity = natation

Page 29

Picture 1 = 1 point
Picture 2 = –3 points
Picture 3 = 2 points
Picture 3 is the winner

Page 31

Suggested answers:
Words which sound like English – la girafe, le bébé, le cousin, grand.
Words which remind you of something – le singe, la poubelle, le gratte-ciel, la petite-fille, la salle de bains.
Words for saying out loud twelve times – le neveu, la bouche, la chambre.
Words for adding to your collection – any or all of the above.
Any answer is acceptable as long as you can say why you thought that.

Page 33

Watch the video of the Tour de France and winter sports in the Alps. It's superb! Go into the kitchen. There is a bottle of wine, some Coca-Cola, some glasses and some cakes on the table.

Pages 34–35 Revision exercises

Exercise 1
a 3　**b** 1　**c** 3　**d** 3

Exercise 2

a Je l'aime.
b Je le (or la) déteste.
c Je ne l'aime pas du tout.
d Je l'aime bien.
e Ce n'est pas bien.

Exerices 3

Suggested answers:

a mort-aux-rats (f) – rat poison (add it to my collection)
b magnifique – magnificent (remember it is similar to English)
c sapin (m) de Noël – christmas tree (say it twelve times)
d bouche (f) – mouth (say it twelve times)
e jouer au rugby – play rugby (remember it is similar to English)

Exercise 4

a garden
b kitchen
c north
d deux
e bras
f sapin

Exercise 5

a It could be a note telling you where something is, or what is going to happen. It may be a reminder. It has probably been left by a member of the family. You may have already recognised the word 'Maman'.
b You may have recognised 'bouteille – bottle, limonade – lemonade, des verres – glasses, sandwichs – sandwiches, au fromage – cheese, football – football, vin rouge – red wine, boulanger – baker, galette des rois – cake for January 6th'.
c You may have guessed 'sur la table – on the table, pour vous – for you, je vais – I'm going, la télé – the telly/TV.
d You may have had to look up 'dans – in, la cave – the cellar, commander – order'.

It actually doesn't matter how many of the words you recognised, how many you guessed and how many you had to look up, or even if you didn't understand all of them, as long as you were able to answer the questions in Exercise 6.

Exercise 6

a on the table
b cheese sandwiches
c there is a football match on the television
d a bottle of red wine
e to the baker's

Page 37

1 jogging
2 football
3 sandwich
4 coca
5 table
6 match
7 keepfit
8 super

Page 39

1 il y a trois semaines
2 il y a
3 il fait noir
4 ça m'est égal
5 depuis deux semaines
6 tout d'un coup
7 il y a trois semaines
8 Chez Marc
9 Tout d'un coup
10 il fait noir
11 Chez le boucher
12 il y a deux semaines
13 je fais du karaté

Missing phrase = il faut rentrer
(it's necessary to go back)

Page 41

Peignez la salle à manger verte. Peignez le salon bleu. Réparez la lampe cassée dans la salle à manger.

Pages 42–43 Revision exercises

Exercise 1

novembre, jogging, keepfit, match, hockey, télé, lettre, pull, bleu, serpent

Exercise 2

a musique
b sandwich
c football
d ski
e super

Exercise 3

a You need to do something – Il faut
b Something happens suddenly – Tout d'un coup
c You are going to Luc's house – Chez Luc
d You are going to the baker's – Chez le boulanger
e You did something three weeks ago – Il y a trois semaines

Exercise 4

a chez
b depuis deux ans
c ça m'est égal
d il y a
e il y a trois ans

Exercise 5

a Peignez
b Changez
c Réparez
d dans
e cassée

Exercise 6

a peindre
b bleue
c réparez
d le
e dans